A TOUGH TALE

A TOUGH TALE

by
**MONGANE
WALLY
SEROTE**

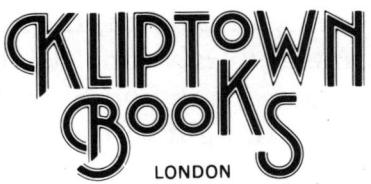

LONDON

FIRST PUBLISHED BY KLIPTOWN BOOKS 1987

ISBN 0 904759 80 6

Printed by Honey Press Limited
Banbury, Oxfordshire

We remember those murdered by the South African fascist army in Luanda, Lusaka, Matola, Maseru, Mbabane and Gaborone. Their blood cements future relations in Southern Africa. And together we shall fight to free Africa from imperialism.

PART ONE

*FOR
HOLES ARE FOREVER COLD AND DARK
AND THEY THREATEN LIFE.*

We want the world to know:
we have come a long way now,
we are not like spotless whiteshirts
we are khakhi
it is the time, the road, the dust, the heat, the
    rain and the wind
which did it all.

in the deep of night
when the heartbeat keeps pace with the
    persistent twinkle of the stars
when we hear the slow pace of the moon
and our breath keeps our eyelids blinking
we listen
we watch with our silent fingers
we page for wisdom through the stubborn night
sleepless we ask:
what is to be patient and to
be stubborn in patience?

We page through each other's faces
we read each looking eye.
it has taken lives to be able to do so.
we move like a tortoise
as we journey home.
home –
where are we that we are not home?
ah
it is a long story this
that is why we page every face
and read each look
and move like a tortoise.

please
spare our tongue, do not make us relate the long
    story
because when your mother goes mad
you would rather help her to sanity than just
    talk about her madness.
we want to help ours—
in this long time of our bewilderment
she's done and shown us the most strange things
so: we stalk her
that is why we are not home.

ah
here comes the day: not like the one we knew
the light here is too bright
and the heat too strong
the sky too vast and weighs heavily on the
    shoulders
we carry it though
one step at a time
we hear each pulse of the heart and each blink
    of the eye
and keep the mind in its shell
we are stubborn
we value life here in this heat under this vast
    sky.
here
under the naked light of the sun
we perch on tree tops, we grow gentle eyes
we turn the nerves of sinews into thin steel
    wires
and merge our voices with the breeze of the
    open air.

here
under this incredible light
we watch the demon
wear many faces and eyes and styles of walking
    and laughter.

ah
we really have come a long way.

we all live here now
in the twilight
where shadows and light bob and weave
twist and try to break each other's necks
here
it gets too cold
or too hot
and at times too wet
or too dry
ah
by watching
and listening
we have all learnt and come to know
that the weather is not good for anyone

here
the footsteps of apartheid
like a red hot iron rod placed on the flesh
has left its footprints,
on infants
on women and mothers
on men and fathers
on children
it has left its marks

on the man in the factories
in the mines
on the man sweeping the streets
on the woman on her knees in a kitchen in a
    factory
on the children at school in the streets
when all of us at last aged and ill
like debris
we were thrown back to the township
to the village
and time, merciless and accomplice
took our life
here we are then
we popped out of life to death
having witnessed the worst
unemployed
jailed and diseased and impoverished
until when the pain of humiliation
like the pain of a raped woman
throbbed and kept pace with our eye-wink
so it was
ah
my friends remember
how we fought each other then
how we killed each other then
how
as if our life were flesh between the teeth of a
    hungry animal
we tore it
with knives
with alcohol
we tore at it making it shreds with rage

why
why my friends
in a land
whose multi-colour wealth bloomed
in a blinding flash
dappling the air which glitter with gold
for whites
while blacks toil
in the factory
where a pin, a screw, a bottle
a bit of iron
whirl on the conveyor belt
which purrs the movement of a wheel
a machine
roaring and roaring and roaring
at times –
machines whistle, or rattle
or buzz
or as we said roar
or make all these sounds
the machines
roaring and rattling, whistling and buzzing
they ask for a finger and then a hand
and then an arm
they pull and pull and pull
they leave holes in the earth
smoke in the sky
oil in the sea and miles and miles of graves
so it is
everywhere and anywhere
ask any worker:
the miners

whose sight like a chameleon
now changes the colour of their stare
now for the light and then for the darkness
and their muscles
when they are asleep
wriggle like those of a horse tired of flies on its
    body
these men
like ants on their busy journeys
end beneath the earth
nibbling it
like rats
they gnaw at it
listening to the dripping drifting water
and the falling sods
and the roaring machines and hammers
which like fire erasing grass
erase all memories of loved ones
for
holes are forever cold and dark
and they threaten life

these men
emerge from the hole
to the sunlight which yields no hope
for it never visits their compound
where other men lie on their backs and stare at
    the asbestos ceiling
as their minds like wailing glass
shatter against the thick cold wall of loneliness.
where is my wife
my children, mother, my father
my brother

oh
my house where we sang, laughed and cried
where is that sun that climbs above the trees
dragging shadows along, around the houses
the trees, moving shadows
strolling along with the cattle, goats and sheep
whose neck bells ring and ring into the dark
        night?
have the children grown up
do the children know where I am
Does Nomafa tell them?
Nomafa
Six months, two years, three years away
when does three years become now?

ah
but that land is so far away, achingly far away
that land
but the land that land
where fleshless cattle, goats and sheep even dogs
        roam
is as dry as a cement slab
it can't seep water
it keeps roots out
the land where goats, sheep and cattle stare
dull
where the children
ill
they cry and cry and cry
yet miraculously, the women, Nomafa
ekes out porridge, spinach and fire from the
        cement slab
and I know:

the truck must come to take me
the train must take me
to the hole
to here
where the rock walls yield to my and the
    machine's singing
where rats squeak
here
where water runs and cries and smells in the
    dark
here
it is hard here
as hard as the Boer's mind and head

ah
but I know
when the song like rain like thunder holds the
    sky
and the footsteps
like the roar of a wild flood
emerge
and we
like fire rear and roll towards the iron gates
on the day of the strike
then
what is it like
it is like being drunk with rage
Yes
it is like being happy
Yes
it is like crying from pain of joy
no—

what is it like, how does one tell it?
it is the distant glitter of freedom at the end of
    this long road.

Something yields during a strike
the Boer
with his hard mind and hard head
knows better
he moves back, not only that
we move out forward
in song
in dance
slowly we move forward
even the songs we sang as boys yield
to new words which must hold our lives
things change
even the Boer moves back only to surge forward
    again
with batons, guns and dogs
with smoke
and we make fire
storm the walls, crush glass, barricade the Boer
    streets
gates
offices
crush his cars
yes, something yields during a strike action
we move out of the compound
we leave it behind with its cold walls
we clear ground and create space
something yields at this hour
beyond the smell of tear gas and gunpowder

beyond the smell of blood
something yields
when police stations yield behind high fences
    and sandbags
and the song says
hold
hold
hold on
the time is here when the Boer laager must
    crumble
ah
the road curls
gets steeper
slopes
is hot with heat
but hold
hold
hold on
soon Botha will yelp
like
Reagan, Thatcher and those others who are an
    issue of their
children's wrath
must yelp
when Pretoria Air Force HQ shatters and sends
    screaming flying glass
around
we have arrived
the people are here, something must yield

ah
by watching

and listening
while gagged and muzzled
we have all come to learn and know
that freedom or the grave.

listen,

once a child sparkled our hopes with its eyes,
its gait
this child
once
would leap into the air like a gemsbok
with laughter which rang of joy
a joy glowing like headlights of a car in the
      night,
a child, Hector, Katryn Schoon
ours
bones, blood and flesh which promised to seize
      the future,
our blood this child
our flesh
our hope,
whose curiosity pins our adult life
us urging it on
it was a promise that the present can be lived,
and then
the bullet came, the bomb
blind
mad with speed and sound
it sprawled the little bones on the dusty street
it spilled and splashed blood on floors and walls
leaving us cold with disbelief—

The weather is bad here:

Sometimes
it feels late here, late for everything
it does;
when blue flames and smoke curl and curve with
        rage in the sky
when the noise cracks and seems to wait a little
        while in the air
and many eyes seem to blink
staring, a second too long
then
it feels late here, late for everything
but
we are men and women
a people whose experience cannot be measured
        with a ruler
we did strike at Pretoria HQ
with anger and precision
remember, oh comrade
that history which ever seemed to discard us
which forever threw us on the banks of the river
taught us
that with warm hearts, and clear minds
with clean hands and unsparing tongues
with eyes which have sight and can see
we can take it in our arms to destroy oppression
        and exploitation
then,
then that is when we can lose those we love
the Lion of Chiawelo
Jenny Schoon

Ruth First
the familiar noise does then, take place
then
we part with wives, sons, daughters, lovers
we part with comrades
men, women, young and old
whose laughter
or tears
or little things they did which make them them
remind us
we were just a little too late
we did not walk out the door in time
or our long partings held us just a little too long
while laughing
or talking
reading or phoning
maybe too long in an embrace with one long
    missed
we overslept
or slept at the wrong minute
and thus gave the enemy a moment
to calculate and time to reach us
Then, I must admit –
our sorrow is as red as blood
the silence comes
the quietness holds us, with its chill
it cuts then, painfully, between the mind and the
    heart
– we expect the enemy to be so –
each of his acts
like rain after a long drought
will leave us, like the landscape –

green
trees sprouting little leaflets
grass being fresh and flowers sprouting

we
we are men and women, children
who have been scattered to different sunsets and
    sunrises
everywhere where we have been,
we watched
listened and asked
learnt
and so steeled our will
we know now
that oppressors are as stubborn as the back of a
    tortoise
that exploiters are as jumpy and as tricky as a
    flea.

yet
we also know
as the roots hold the tree
and the sun or the moon light the earth
or the earth moves to make time
so are we
hundreds
thousands of us, millions
move
and will make change
it is our hands, legs, eyes and ears
which hold
walk

see and hear
for the oppressor and exploiter,
we shift, as the earth does, in Mdantsane
in Sebokeng
Huhudi
Grahamstown,
in Johannesburg we shift our hands
legs,
eyes
and ears
slowly
we move as the Movement
to the day and night
when we will hold, walk, see and hear for our
      land and us
through fire
and rhythmic sound of the gun which bites into
      the enemy's marrow
we shift
we gnaw and nibble at the enemy
we learn in the while, to unite
for that the oppressor is as stubborn as facts
is a fact
we eat him then as worms do a carcass
in unity
song
and fire
we penetrate with teeth of a fish
through the skin
past the nerve
to the bone and spill the marrow
ah

our land knows no peace
the one time master
and the one time slave
eye each other
spend sleepless nights in watch
we sleep with our boots on—
in my country
men, women young and old
dream dreams
know the loud noise of nightmares
as we say—
we want no war
we did not want to spill blood
or to shatter anyone's dreams
but if that is the height of freedom
ah
look,
we shall climb it slowly
minute for minute
stone for stone
as Mandela said and,
as Mahlangu said
the price of this freedom spills from our pores
is sipped by our land or lands where we have
      been
as it does
as we die
our eye
as stubborn as the twinkle of a star
we rivet it on the future
where all will be equal
to make life

to make history
to make culture
to be part of peace loving man
so our eye stares
let's tell anyone who hates what we say,
that
our rage is as red as furious flames
our courage
must mount wounds and walk this earth
so it takes
to be able to make children
talk and laugh
cry with them
hold them by the hand
see them—
learn to dismount the bed,
walk the floor
make sounds and first words of their lives
that's what it takes to see our children
smile
ask
walk out into the open sun and wind
and
come back to ask and give their opinions
as they teach us
with arms and smiles and sight which flails and
    flies
telling us the simple things of life

ah
remember
the ghettos and villages we grew in

not like birds
not like trees
not like ants
nor even like day and night
here
we grew, watching the old disintegrate
yet
strong like steel in their words
warning of days to come or days which are here
shaped by apartheid oppression and exploitation
today we mount the words of the old
they are everything
simple
they say life rejects oppression
we mount them
as if we tame tigers
we mount them as does one who wriggles in
        water
trying to hold and learning that water can't be
        held
we mount the words till we can swim

we want the world to know
we have come a long long way
mounting the bluntness of the chilly winter
        night
mounting the sharp edge of the hot summer day
it is a long story this —
told
by long hours of prison days
when Fischer dies of cancer in jail
when a young man and Thandi Modise

24

face the steel door and thick cement walls
feel the flesh from their nerves
and hail: 'Amandla!'
and the silence is then measured in years
which
as the autumn wind takes leaves off trees
takes the youth–years of these comrades –
yes
some of our young
having turned their bloody hearts into courage
mounted time and the wind
chose through their brave acts graves anywhere
on the road
in the river
in cells or dying stared at by trees and cruel
    eyes
and got time to hail 'Amandla!'
leaving behind one simple truth:
in my country –
Victory is certain!

Victory for what?
this victory red with blood of children of
    unknown mothers
Tambo
victory for what?
ah
we have come a long way indeed!
we must as we look this victory in the eye,
mount the wound
mount the minute
walk the road stone for stone

conscious
we come from a long past
from a long time
from minutes which were pages of a book
written through united screams
about a great continent filled with treachery at
    times
so began our bloody war my friends
a long time gone and we ask:
victory
victory for what Mabhida?
our sight is steady
it must be.
our steps are slow and conscious here
they must be.
our hand is easy but it can be firm
it must be.
So our journey is made, as we eye victory
a victory we know was also bloody
it was, we knew it would be so
we eye it
as the sky once watched the Sasol flames rage
we eyed victory
not so long ago,
when the children
mounted the old wounds
creating smoke, fire and ash
creating debris
of beerhalls
trains
buses
Bantu Affairs Commissioners' Offices

creating corpses
of councillors, informers and puppets
articulating
with eloquence and precision
that
oppression negates life, that united
the exploited have the might of floods
and so
the women mounted the pus–filled wound
the workers
in Tembisa
Sebokeng, Grahamstown, Katlehong, Cape Town
in Durban
the flood leaped and surged forward.

ah

the day here is not like the one we once knew
we mount wounds here
conscious
we hold hands
workers, schoolchildren, women
we build barricades and bridges
make fire, sing songs
surge
dream dreams
move in Movement
for
on the palms of our hands, like a warm egg
a new world will crack the shell
will emerge

In my country
the smoke still curls and heaves to the sky
tongues of flame leap and make the sky mauve
the noise can still be heard,
glass still wails and wails and wails
amidst this
Tambo's voice is heard calling –
let the new men and women emerge
amidst this
Botha's voice is heard calling –
tear gas, rubber bullets, Hippos and Casspirs
mow down children, women and men
while Reagan smiles
and Thatcher grins
let them,
the friendship presents they give the Boers
are death makers for us
let them be friends.

if it were that we do not know that
or have not seen
the sun rise the moon set
seasons come and pass
if it were that we did not know
that time like science is honest
we would cry like pained children
but since we know these
we ask
even as the memory sometimes fails
or the body ails
we ask
even as we watch from the trench

terror howling like a cat gone mad
under the blue open sky
we ask
how can there be pus unless there's a wound?
we have told our tale
in blood
we will wait as time unfolds
and we hold it in the palms of our hands
for we are gods
who make children
who make the hour of the day
whose word will be final about our destiny
so it is
if you listen to the wind
and look at the sun or moon
if you can
and you watch the day unfold
and the night unroll its shadows
you have heard the footsteps of god
and have seen love of life
whose birth
is blood –
flesh torn to shreds and spilled on thorn tree
     branches
flesh and blood smudged on brick walls
So Africa
your children who love life
who know the terror of loneliness
who make demands on their hands
legs
eyes
ears

to make them friends with freedom –

They come young
motherless
they speak of rubber bullets and birdshots
they speak of young fresh blood spilled in the
    streets
these children of a restless hour
now unfold
peel off
they wear steel threads for nerves
can you hear their rolling footsteps
can you hear their songs
their youth which is enraged by oppression
is the blood of struggle
these children are ageless
women and men
some had not as yet finished being children
others though long ripe, are unable to be
    mothers or fathers
wives or husbands
they've responded, body and soul to the restless
    hour
to turn its unlivable moments
to a livable present
through their flesh and blood
by shattering ignorance
and by pain of sleepless nights
step by step
stone for stone
minute by minute
we pierce the mind once woolled by oppression

we tear apart poverty and squalor
and we search for the new man and the new
　　woman
in us—
for my country must be rebuilt.
ah
how do I tell this long tale?
that workers in my country march and fight
from within mines and factories
from within mealie-fields, fruit orchards and
　　wheat fields
they march
from within despicable ghettoes and villages
from out the Bantustans and prisons
no longer with simplicity from ignorance
but they are simple of word
and so the little girls and boys
they emerge from out of an unripe youth
to mount the restless hour
they are freedom children.

There is no way this tale can be told
by a little man like me
it is a tale
fresh every minute and every hour
it is a gurgle tale of blood
a fugue
it is a tale of deaths died in strange ways and
　　places
it is told by flashes of purple, yellow and green
　　smoke and flames
flying in the sky, devouring hate

it is a tale told by running footsteps at night
this tale
is told in the streets of my town
in the alleys of the night hour
it is told by the surge of masses of people
in bright daylight speaking of the darkest
      moments of their lives
which seek an out, into the bright hour.

this tale is long
it is told by the stealth and skill
of young men and women who spend hours
      alone
whose patience is like the twinkle of a star in
      the dark night
which glitters an eternal stare
these little ones
are the eye of a people at war,
their blood is the life of our struggle
I said
how does one tell a tale this tough!
my people
I cannot be rash with this tale
you taught me to wait and to be patient
so you —
through your wealth of life
you tell this tale as your life unfolds.

PART TWO
LIFE IS FREEDOM

Our past is measured through fresh graves
they scatter along footpaths
ravines and near rivers
where we drank when we were thirsty.
Our death-beds are streets we walk daily.

So is our tale.

Our tale good friends you read from sandy paths
from brown grass blades
from everywhere where most people would shy
    to die
this is our tale
of sleepless little boys and girls
who have moved from one country to the other
but never theirs
for
there hounds howl with a piercing loud howl
and crickets chirp
from mouths, tongues, ears and eyes of corpses
everywhere where there should have been life,
    but where it is not
there they chirp
so do spider webs hang and dangle
wait and rear
stir just a little for maybe, just maybe, life may
    loom.

So is our tale.
Our past is measured through searching for
    hands to shake and
shoulders
to hug

Under this sun
whose heat rings and rings and rings like the
        sharpest point of a spear
ready to be planted on a rib cage
so that a tale could end
but we then said, for the whole world to hear,
at every end there we begin.
Our tale is endless.
What is the point someone may ask
for us to count grass blades where our blood was
        spilled
or countries where some of our best lie buried
or even seek those paths which are scattered
        with our graves
what, is the point?
yes,
there is no point I say
for
here at the end we begin
for it takes two to fight
we fought and fell
and fight
for it is in this bloody fight that we learnt
that for freedom death deserves contempt.

Our tale is that there are many types of death,
remember
how as if honesty were a nut
how with a stone with rough urges we crushed
        it against another stone
how as children our parents bought birth
        certificates and names for us
house numbers and school passages for us

how they looked us in the eye
warning
the future has been empty for us
let what limb or bone crack or break
but the future for you must be different, *must* be
    better
ah
what did they not do to say it must be so?
their youth broke
and like mud wrinkles took their faces
like a crumbling cake their back broke and bent
    as we watched
their eyes now grey were also glassy
their gait slow
they seemed to wait forever now
so did the places we grew in
where the house I was born stood, now stands
    tall wobbly grass
the streets I used to walk
are like dry beds, scattered with coke and fanta
    tins
I do not know where my relatives are,
nor do I know where my friends are
so in distant lands we forged comrades.

Why does one want to tell such a gory tale?
so that, my friends, our past is not erased.

Before my parents, I remember
there were the old men and women
whose bodies had been wrung by age
whose hands and legs were as hard as steel
    holding skyscrapers

who now and then seemed puzzled by the
        present
and so were watchful
careful
in the way they held our hands
as they whispered about what they had known
        and what they saw
also,
they seemed to stand aside with a wise look in
        their faces
for struggle
like stone and steel rubbing together,
leaves steel a little sharper.

Ah
in my old age or near it
when my youth days and games are gone
as it is now
when changes have hammered innocence out of
        me
as I said, there are many types of death
and in my young days I saw most of them,
staring into my eye
and the sky remained blank giving no
        explanation
nor pity
until when the past in eloquence said, walk on
        we shall see
we have walked into many dark alleys in that
        past
and here we are today.

This is not and must not be a sad tale
it cannot be
it is a song whose strength like strong wind
can blow and reveal our weaknesses
for that we must know.
remember
and this lovers must know better
how
when a heart is broken the mind searches and
        searches
for something to hold on to
to rest its weariness
and so gather strength for the broken heart
yes
even that has to be done with skill
find the strong branch to hang from for the
        weak one can break
and where, where would the poor heart be?
we know all this and more
and yet this time asks: *really*?
yes we do
for our future is a poem which says so.
my friends,
today we are watching a mamba spit and strike,
        wink and whistle
and strike
at times blandly
and the old man, laughing, I watching him, says
        it must be so
the snake has gone mad
we made him so, we found his hold and struck
        him

he knows we want his head now.
Ah
now, I look at the mad mamba with a different
    eye
and as I have said
I can no longer be innocent.

It is not because I am landless that I am no
    longer an innocent child
the story of my land is known by all
the old people have told it to me too in whispers
    at times
when other people offered their land to us
or when they treated us like dogs for we had
    none
I learnt to look at my distant land
and to get near to it
through song and dance and poem
and through the letting of blood every part of
    me scratching for space in it
with grenade at hand I claim it
look how far we have gone now
did no one know we had no land, why
    couldn't they help me talk to claim it?
I hear the Palestinian child sing this song
the Nicaraguan
a child in the Sahara sings also
a song which is very familiar
our past and present are measured in fresh
    graves
scattered along riverbeds and ravines
as I tell this tale

newspapers TVs and radios count our dead daily
innocence used to tell me the world would be
    shocked
but Reagan and Thatcher tell me otherwise
yet hope rings in me
like a twinkling star
in the dark of night.

yes, so is our tale.

It is a tale that mounts on stubborn hope
this time has told us to be owls that fly in
    daylight
we do so
also
fingerless and toeless we climb the mountain,
    someone must know this.
This is an ageless tale
told through many lives from villages, farms,
    factories and streets
it is a tale which makes some want to be deaf or
    blind
to us
it is a tale asking
how tall is peace?
And now I look at my country, ravaged by
    raging fire
bullets and bombs savage my country
and voices echo above all this noise
of crushing thunder, of thunder angry and
    tireless
and again the old man is there

grimacing, yet
tired
smiling and at times a little surprised
he stands there
and he and the old lady talk
look
talk
seek me in this noise
they whisper
as we move in and out of the thunder
sometimes some are left behind, lost
I look at the old faces
same
sometimes we come back from within more in
     number
I look at the old faces
same
sometimes no one comes back
I look at the old faces
same – the Movement
an unflinching eye
sometimes a smile
a tear
a questioning face
but that unflinching eye is there staring
and the even voice
of the machine of the wind of water of the sea of
     the sky
the even voice
our tale my friends
you read from the movement of the experienced
     lips

the noise of the mines
of the farms
of the factories
the voice that stood the test of crushing
        experience
keeps asking:
if fire can rage so fiercely, how tall is peace?
our tongues and our fingers are scalpels to carve
        peace
please believe me
if you do
you and I will build peace here
shaped by corpses cut by raging bullets and
        thunderous bombs
of mad men
killing workers, students, women, children
        mercilessly for their greed
we shall circle them
watch the fear and madness in their eyes
we watch
singing one with the voice of time
we watch
grenade and gun in hand
we march

one morning
my people will hang on a sunrise
as a child after falling would to its mother;
the morning
we shall stand face to face with the sun
like a woman would
who has been raped and raped and raped

a woman whose eyes will stare
whose face will be there without expression
for indeed
many words, many deeds and many things
shall have lost their old meanings;
we shall stand face to face with the sun
we shall hang on a sunrise
perch on the dawn of a day
leaving behind us
so many dead
wounded
mad
so many senseless things
we shall have buried Apartheid –
how shall we look at each other then,
how shall we shake hands,
how shall we hug each other that day?
ah
how shall we smile and laugh
what first words will we utter?
We are a wounded people
so many nights
have we huddled into our dark night
hurt
crying
learning to fight anew
so many nights –
what shall we look like when that sunrise
    comes?
what shall we do with its first minute
first hour
first day?

I ask my people
for we have said 'South Africa belongs to all
    who live in it. . .'
I ask my people
for it is with our having been used to the smell
    of blood
that we wrote through lives taken by bullets
that
to have food, a home and a job is not a favour;
my people
I ask
for it is you through song
dancing feet
clenched fists who shall have made walls tumble
and made empires to shrivel
like an inflated balloon, pierced –
it shall be you
who send the workers and peasants the masses
    into the corridors of power
it shall be us with power in our hands;
what shall we do that day,
I ask the Freedom Charter
how shall we walk the street
what gait will carry us
I ask?
I read the eye of an MK soldier
I read the face of an ANC cadre
I read their gait
their clenched fists
I hear their song and slogan
I listen to the wind sun and moon
ah

look at me
I can smile even laugh!
my people
how shall we hold that long awaited day?
I ask *now*
as gunsmoke, tear gas and blood smell
as we sing, dance and fight
I ask now my people,
as day in day out
we spent sleepless nights
we walk
days filled with peril
I ask now
as our rulers send small boys
to kill our children
to burn our homes
to rape our wives, sisters and daughters
I ask you now
while you are so wounded
so bloodied in war
what shall we do on that day?
you smile?
I smile
how can I not when so many times I saw
comrades pick up a gun from another who just
    fell
while the gun still is as warm as a bed just
    vacated?
I smile
for I have listened to comrades talk about our
    future
they made me nostalgic for peace

I smile
for every day so many people in the world agree
that our bloody battle is just,
I smile
for daily the oppressor and exploiter
goes mad and madder
I smile
for our red hearts are daily
with each falling comrade
a symbol of hatred for oppression and
        exploitation
how can I not smile
when I look at the Africans
Coloureds
Indians
whites
and know that one day we shall be one people
South Africans
with power in our hands, using it to build
        peace?
how can I not smile
when we shall sing a Nkosi Sikelela iAfrika
under a
black
green
and gold flag
which we chose?
I smile
for war shall have taught us
and Africa shall have taught us
and the world shall have taught
that equality of a people

is a firm foundation for progress.
me I smile my friend
for in my country
through struggle, through great pain
through knowledge
the masses defend and built the ANC
the workers defend and built Sactu
the masses, the workers, the students, the
    learned
defend and built the ANC, Sactu and the SACP
with many painful days
which
like the hour-arm on a clock
takes time to come and go,
we organise ourselves
and so engrave hope and optimism
on our future

London, April 1987